IMAGES
of America

RUBY'S INN AT BRYCE CANYON

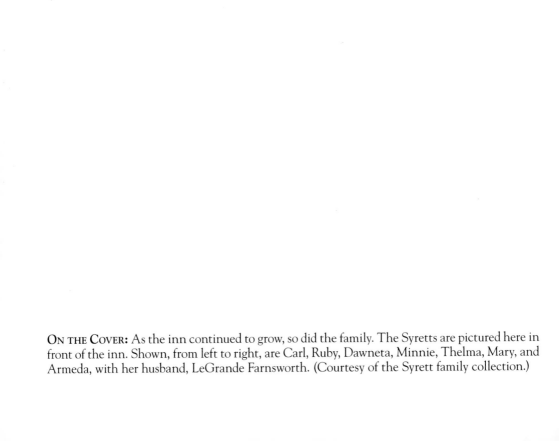

IMAGES
of America

RUBY'S INN AT BRYCE CANYON

A. Jean Seiler

ARCADIA
PUBLISHING

Published by Arcadia Publishing
Charleston, South Carolina

Printed in the United States of America

Library of Congress Control Number: 2013934396

For all general information, please contact Arcadia Publishing:
Telephone 843-853-2070
Fax 843-853-0044
E-mail sales@arcadiapublishing.com
For customer service and orders:
Toll-Free 1-888-313-2665

Visit us on the Internet at www.arcadiapublishing.com

To Ruby and Minnie Syrett, who had the vision of what Bryce
Canyon would become. To their hard work and example that can
be seen today as visitors from around the world are welcomed
to Ruby's Inn. Finally, to this beautiful part of the world that
has an indescribable draw for those who visit and those who
are fortunate enough to call Bryce Canyon their home.

CONTENTS

ACKNOWLEDGMENTS

I would like to thank the Syrett family for sharing their stories and photographs to make this book possible—especially Roderick K. and Kathern Syrett for their encouragement and commitment to seeing this project through. A thank-you goes to Armeda (Syrett) Farnsworth and Jean (Bybee) Syrett for their dedication in telling the story of Ruby and Minnie and preserving so many of the details of the early days of Bryce Canyon, as well as to Daniel Davis with the Utah State University Photograph Archives for the Dr. W.H. Hopkins image scans. Harold Excell, a nephew of Ruby and Minnie, discovered and preserved many of the Hopkins photographs. Bryce Canyon National Park provided access to its archives and history associated with this early period. I would also like to recognize the many friends, neighbors, and employees of the Syrett family, who have helped from the very beginning to make Ruby's Inn what it is today. Thanks go to Arcadia Publishing for its commitment to capturing the images and stories across America to be enjoyed by future generations. Finally, I must thank Stacia, our acquisitions editor, and my wife, Spring, for keeping me on task to complete this project. This is but a small part of the continuing story of Bryce Canyon and its people. The photographs in this book are courtesy of the Syrett family collection, which was formed from family images and donations of photographs by Hal Rumel and Dr. W.H. Hopkins.

INTRODUCTION

The early story of Bryce Canyon is the story of a land that lay undiscovered and protected by its remoteness in the wilds of Southern Utah. In October 1776, Franciscan friars Atanasio Dominguez and Silvestre Velez de Escalante came close enough to view the Pink Cliffs of the Paunsaugunt Plateau to the north as they searched for a crossing of the Colorado River. Jedediah Smith, George Yount, and John C. Fremont all explored around the plateau regions as they searched for routes to California. Mormon scouts were sent in 1852 to explore the Sevier River regions, including what is now Circleville and Panguitch. Their trail offered them a view of the Sunset Cliffs on the western side of the Paunsaugunt Plateau. In 1866, a group of Indian fighters from St. George followed a course to the upper Paria Valley, which afforded them views of the great amphitheaters of Bryce Canyon. In 1879, Maj. John Wesley Powell, working as a surveyor for the US Geological Survey, visited the south end of the plateau, presenting a view of the so-called Grand Staircase of geological steps reaching all the way to the Grand Canyon.

Water was scarce in these high mountain valleys, and communities developed along the available water sources. Irrigation projects were organized to distribute water to the farms, and soon, most of the farmland was being cultivated. Ranchers began exploring the surrounding mountains in search of suitable land for grazing and harvesting of timber. They had left their homes in Europe to join other dedicated Saints in the new territory of Utah. These determined early settlers prepared the way for future generations who would call Utah's Canyon Country their home.

Since that humble beginning, millions of visitors have come to experience the splendor and vastness of this unique landscape and meet the people who still call this land their home.

One

HOMESTEADING

The first of many Mormon pioneers arrived in the Salt Lake Valley in July 1847. Almost immediately, Brigham Young sent scouting parties throughout the Utah Territory to discover suitable lands to settle and farm. Many families, after arriving from Europe, were sent to establish new communities throughout the West. Ebenezer Bryce, a convert from Scotland, and his wife, Mary, were sent to St. George, Utah, to help build the Mormon temple. Ebenezer used his skills as a shipbuilder and carpenter to operate the steam-powered sawmill that provided the needed lumber. In 1875, Ebenezer, Mary, and their 10 children moved from St. George to the upper Paria Valley and built a log home at the base of the canyon that would later bear his name. Times were hard for those early pioneer families. The need to provide shelter, food, and safety occupied all of their days. Little time was left to ponder the beauties that surrounded them. In an oft-quoted and understated description of the canyon, Ebenezer was said to simply say it (the canyon) was "a hell of a place to lose a cow." Ebenezer moved his family from this famous canyon long before it was discovered by the nearly 1.5 million tourists who visit each year from all around the world.

The story begins in the spring of 1916 when Reuben "Ruby" and Minnie Syrett left their home in Panguitch, Utah, and ventured to the edge of the Paunsaugunt Plateau to homestead a quarter section of land and build their ranch. Little did they realize how the decision to move would affect their lives and the lives of generations of their family yet to come.

Ebenezer Bryce, an early convert to the Mormon Church, was born in Scotland. He studied to become a carpenter and shipbuilder in his native land prior to immigrating to the United States in 1848. He married Mary Ann Park in Salt Lake City in April 1854, and they eventually became the parents of 12 children. They moved to St. George to help with the construction of the Mormon temple. He was asked to build a chapel in Pine Valley, and because of his shipbuilding skills, he modeled the building after an upside-down ship. His structure remains as the oldest continuously used chapel of the Church of Jesus Christ of Latter-day Saints (LDS).

In 1876, Ebenezer, Mary, and their 10 children relocated to the upper Paria Valley in Garfield County, Utah. They settled with several other families in an area they named Clifton ("cliff town") because of the prominent Pink Cliffs to the east of the valley. Ebenezer helped build irrigation channels and made it possible to raise crops and livestock. This photograph shows the remains of their log home. It has since been relocated to the town of Tropic, Utah. Ebenezer had moved his family in hopes of a milder climate for his wife's health. By 1880, they decided to leave Clifton and move to Arizona.

Ruby Syrett and Minnie Excell Syrett are pictured here on their wedding day, July 7, 1905. The Syretts and Excells were true descendents of Mormon pioneers. Their parents were converts from England. The Syrett family built their home in Kingston, and the Excell family moved to Panguitch. Both of these villages were located in the Sevier River Valley. The Syretts became acquainted as their families socialized together. Ruby learned the trades of millwright and ranching.

Seen here, the Syrett family home in Panguitch is where they began their married life together. Their son Carl and daughter Armeda were born here. During this time in their lives, Ruby helped his father and brother operate the flour mills in Kingston and Panguitch. Minnie took care of the home, making rag rugs, canning, and providing for the needs of their small family. Ruby and Minnie had six children, four of whom died in infancy.

In May 1916, six weeks after the birth of their daughter Armeda, Ruby and Minnie Syrett took their family and traveled the 26 miles from Panguitch to an area near the rim of Bryce Canyon. It was here that they had picked to homestead. Travel was rough, as roads were almost nonexistent. They traveled to the top of Red Canyon the first day, left their wagon, and finished the trip to their new home in a white-topped buggy. They had to return the next day to retrieve the wagon, which contained all of their possessions.

Ruby and Minnie Syrett were determined to do what they had to do to make a success of their new homestead. They had the resources for building a small cabin, as they had located their new home next to a good supply of ponderosa pines. This provided them with building materials and fuel for those first few seasons on the high plateau. Ruby is seen standing in the wagon that carried their belongings to their new home.

Workhorses, cattle, and pigs were among the animals that were found on the Syrett ranch. Minnie was responsible for the cheese-making and involved Carl and Armeda as soon as they were old enough to help with the stirring. They produced a 35-pound cheese each day and used it to barter for flour and produce in the surrounding communities. This skill proved very beneficial when they began to welcome visitors to Bryce Canyon.

According to Ruby Syrett, "It was six weeks after we settled at the ranch, Claude Sudweeks, a cousin and rancher from Tropic, stopped for a neighborly chat. He asked us if we had seen Bryce's Canyon. I said, No, what is it? Claude replied, Oh, just a hole in the ground, but you should see it. One Sunday afternoon, after my neighbors had helped me build a bridge over the Tropic Canal,

my family and I climbed into our white-topped buggy and went to see this 'hole in the ground.' We stood speechless: the coloring, the rock formations, we had never seen anything like it. What a surprise the hole turned out to be! We thought everyone should see it, so from that time on we took our friends there, and we told everyone we met about Bryce."

Ruby Syrett had been taught in his youth to care for and appreciate animals. He taught his children these same values. He believed it was a good way to teach them responsibility.

About this same time, J.W. Humphrey was assigned to manage the Sevier Forest. When he arrived in Panguitch, he began an effort to become familiar with the forest. One of his rangers, Elias Smith, suggested he should see Bryce's Canyon. Humphrey did not express much interest but Smith insisted. When Humphrey came to the rim, he was overwhelmed. He is quoted in Nicholas Scrattish's *History Resource Study: Bryce Canyon National Park*: "You can perhaps imagine my surprise at the indescribable beauty that greeted us, and it was sundown before I could be dragged from the canyon view. You may be sure that I went back the next morning to see the canyon once more, and to plan in my mind how this attraction could be made accessible to the public."

In the summer of 1917, Oliver J. Grimes, official photographer of the *Salt Lake Tribune*, visited Bryce Canyon. When he returned, an article entitled "Utah's New Wonderland" appeared in the Sunday magazine section of the *Tribune* dated August 25, 1918. The article is very positive about the opportunity to travel from Salt Lake by automobile and enjoy the wonders of Bryce Canyon. It even includes detailed directions from Panguitch to the plateau rim:

0.0 miles- Leave Panguitch on the Kanab road.
7.3 miles- Road forks, turn left and cross river (the Sevier)
18.2 miles- Road forks at corral on right; turn right and, at
20.0 miles- Gate—Go through it; (I didn't and got lost).
24.8 miles- Bryce's Canyon.

One Sunday morning in 1919, Ruby and Minnie Syrett were told of a large crowd coming from Salt Lake to see the canyon. According to Minnie, "They wanted us to take a lunch up there and feed them. So we set up a tent and served them." The group was so taken with what they saw, they asked if it would be possible to stay there that night. Ruby went back to the ranch, loaded five or six beds and food for dinner. They slept under the pines and were treated to a large breakfast the next morning.

Folks just kept coming. Ruby set up tent houses for the tourists to sleep in, and the Syretts continued to prepare meals for their guests. This occupied their time from the spring until the fall, allowing almost no time to take care of the ranch.

Word of this beautiful canyon was beginning to spread. Roads were getting better, and people continued to come. The Syretts were being encouraged by their friends to build accommodations that were more permanent for their guests. This occupied their thoughts throughout the winter as they began to prepare for the next year's visitors. The people in this photograph are unidentified.

Two

TOURISTS REST

By the spring of 1919, the Syretts had decided to build a tourist lodge on the rim of the canyon. They had secured a verbal approval from the Utah State Land Board, as the location was on state land, not Forest Service property. They determined they would build a lodge using local timber and stone. They also filed for water rights next to their lodge to assure adequate water for this new enterprise.

Rustic lodgings such as this were popular with the adventurous travelers that were making their way over primitive roads through remote parts of the West to embrace the wonders of nature. The next three years set in motion the events that led Ruby and Minnie Syrett to become true pioneers in Utah's tourism industry.

Early in the spring of 1919, Ruby began construction of the first lodging facility at Bryce Canyon. It measured 30 feet by 71 feet, with a large stone fireplace in the dining hall. The building also included bedrooms for the family, a kitchen, and a storeroom. This log structure became known as Tourists Rest.

Local workers were hired, and work progressed quickly on the new lodge. The setting was close to the rim and just southeast of where the Bryce Canyon Lodge is now located. Ruby also built eight or ten tent houses to accommodate the growing number of overnight visitors coming to see Bryce.

Construction continued throughout the summer season. Lumber was obtained at local sawmills set up in the adjoining forest, logs were cut nearby, and stonework was done by local masons with materials that were gathered on-site.

Water was collected for the lodge from a spring near the rim of the canyon. It was piped to a barrel where it was stored and available throughout the day. One of the comforts provided for the guests was a large hollowed-out log that Ruby had made so his guests could have a hot bath. Many stories were shared about that hollowed-log bathtub.

Each year brought more visitors. Ruby welcomed each of them and made them feel at home.

Those first years at Tourists Rest afforded Ruby and Minnie the opportunity to learn the hotel business. At first, they did not have a way for a guest to register, so many of the visitors were invited to write or carve their names into the large doors at the entrance to the lodge.

Holidays were extraspecial at Bryce Canyon. Celebrations brought visitors and locals together to enjoy the natural surroundings and become acquainted with one another. Ruby always took the time to make these events special. Races, games, and large bonfires could be counted on.

A large open-air dance pavilion was constructed to provide evening activity. It measured 35 feet by 76 feet and was made of ponderosa pine logs. It had benches around the outside walls to afford seating. Local entertainment was provided, and dances lasted well into the night.

This gathering shows Ruby and Minnie with their son Carl on the left and their daughter Armeda in the swing. Ruby built the swing by putting a log between two trees in front of the lodge. Guests enjoyed this touch and took turns in the swing.

This c. 1922 image of Tourists Rest shows Ruby (left), J.W. Humphrey (center), and Carl (far right), with an unidentified visitor seated in the center. Note that the construction of the porch allowed the trees to remain. A close look reveals a flag attached to the top of the tallest tree.

This early advertising postcard was used to promote Tourists Rest and encourages visitors to come to Bryce Canyon The tent houses are visible to the right, as is the famous swing in the center of the photograph.

Travel to Bryce Canyon was always a challenge in those early days. Roads were rough at best, services were nonexistent, and other travelers were few and far between. One always had to be prepared. Tires were a constant problem and had to be repaired on a frequent basis. For many city dwellers, this just added to the spirit of adventure.

Growing up at Bryce Canyon meant always being with the tourists. Armeda is pictured in a rare quiet moment with her father Ruby. There was always much to be done, and Carl and Armeda were taught at a young age that their efforts were important to the success of their parents' business.

Carl Syrett (left) and an unidentified friend enjoy some time to explore Bryce Canyon and be tourists. Carl was old enough to be of great help at Tourists Rest. Stocking the wood for the kitchen and fireplace, getting the water, and helping show the guests to their cabins were daily chores during the summer season. This was in addition to helping Ruby at the ranch, which was three and a half miles away.

Hiking in Bryce Canyon was a favorite pastime for tourists. These early visitors were, by necessity, a hardy bunch. They were often on their own to explore the geological features of the canyons. Routinely, they used streambeds, cattle trails, and the logical routes to get a closer look.

Access below the rim of the canyon was dangerous in those early days. Safe trails needed to be constructed. Maps, guidebooks, and signs were yet to be available. Ruby is shown in this photograph using a ladder to access the top of the canyon. Note that he is carrying a rope and helping his dog Nickel up the ladder.

Friends often traveled together to enjoy the canyon. The effort to hike the canyon frequently required rest stops to admire what was being seen. Bryce Canyon is situated at between 8,000 feet to almost 10,000 feet. For tourists coming from lower elevations, it requires some time to adjust.

These hikers are shown on their return from observing the hoodoos below the rim. They will soon be reminded that descending below the canyon rim eventually requires climbing back out. Fortunately, the higher elevations also provide cooler temperatures during the long summer days.

Most folks preferred staying on their feet, making their own trails to the formations they wanted to see up close. The abundance of one-of-a-kind geological formations caused tourists to attach names to what they saw. Many were in the eye of the beholder, with names such as Temples of the Gods, Queen Victoria, Sinking Ship, and the most well-known, Thor's Hammer.

Some visitors preferred riding to hiking. Ruby kept horses available for these guests and often accompanied them as a guide. Because of the lack of established trails, all one had to do was head to the next landmark and continue exploring the mysteries of the canyon.

The people seen in several of these early images are interesting to wonder about, as many are unidentified. Often, the group is shown with two ladies and one man, two horses and one rider, or one horse and no rider, allowing for the missing person who brought the camera.

This is a classic image of what could be seen below the rim of Bryce Canyon. This photograph was reproduced over the years as a postcard. In the early years, these postcards were colored by hand—an impossible task for an artist who had never witnessed Bryce Canyon firsthand.

The Natural Bridge is another classic image used to advertise the wonders of Bryce Canyon. What makes this photograph unique is the rider and his dog on the top of the narrow rock formation. One can only imagine what a park ranger would say today if someone attempted to duplicate this picture. Again, this image was made into a hand-colored postcard and distributed by visitors throughout the world.

Ruby often guided tourists on horseback to the Red Canyon area just west of Bryce Canyon. This canyon was on the primitive road that took visitors from the Panguitch-Kanab main road to Bryce Canyon. In the beginning, it was no more than a wagon road traveling up the wash bed to the top of the plateau.

Red Canyon has similar scenery to that of Bryce Canyon. What made it unique to the visitor was the contrast of black lava flowing on the west and the clear red formations that gave the canyon its name. Red Canyon provides the gateway to the top of the Paunsaugunt Plateau.

In the early days, hikers had to pick their way through the sagebrush to get close to the hoodoos of Red Canyon. The elevation is lower in this canyon, and a variety of vegetation not seen in the higher regions of Bryce can be found.

As evident in this photograph, roads were primitive, and directions were sparse. This picture looks north on the plateau with Red Canyon to the west (left) and Bryce canyon five miles to the east. It seems that even the tourists were recruited to help give directions.

Snow in the high plateaus could come early in the fall and sometimes last late into the spring. A few folks braved the elements and still visited the canyon. Some would snowshoe or hike, while others would venture into the canyon on skis.

Ruby was always willing to welcome visitors, even when the snow was on the ground. He provided lodging and meals, as well the warmth of the fireplace, at Tourists Rest.

Ruby enjoyed getting out with his guests and exploring the mysteries of the canyon. He is seen in this winter image posing with one of the many unique hoodoos found below the Bryce Canyon rim.

Snow often comes early to the high plateaus, and when it does, the tourists disappear. That was when the lodge was closed for the winter, and the Syrett family went back to their ranch. Often, they would move to the warmer climates of Tropic or Escalante until the spring thaw. Livestock was moved, and work was found helping Ruby's brother run the flour mill.

Some say that Bryce Canyon is at its best in the winter. All of the vibrant colors are accented with a covering of white, powdery snow. This is when the forces of nature are working to enhance the formations of the canyon. The temperature rises above freezing during the day and allows the snow to melt, seep into the millions of cracks in the formations of Bryce, and freeze again during the very cold nights. This continual freezing and thawing is what has helped sculpt Bryce Canyon into what one sees today.

This image was captured in the fall of 1923. It had been three years since Ruby and Minnie decided to build Tourists Rest. They had labored with dedication and love to establish the first lodging facilities at Bryce Canyon. Now, in the fall of the year, they looked back with fond memories of the many visitors they had served and lifelong friends they had made. They also looked forward to the opportunities that lay ahead as they returned home to their ranch.

Three

BACK TO THE RANCH

The fall of 1923 found Ruby and Minnie leaving their beloved Tourists Rest for the last time. That same year, the lands that now comprise Bryce Canyon National Park were designated as a national monument. The Union Pacific Railroad incorporated its subsidiary, the Utah Parks Company, to be the concessionaire providing services to the guests coming to the new parks. Wanting to develop facilities in Bryce, it talked to the Utah Land Board and was told it would need to negotiate with Ruby to procure his holdings at the canyon. They finally agreed on a $10,000 payment to Ruby for the lodge and his water rights.

Ruby and Minnie were convinced that an opportunity was theirs to provide the necessary services and hospitality to those visitors coming to see Bryce's Canyon. That winter, they made plans, and in the spring, construction began on the new inn that would bear Ruby's name and become known worldwide.

The first tourist facilities constructed at Ruby and Minnie's homestead, dating to about 1924, are shown. Their property was located next to what would become the new national park. With the experience they had gained at their lodge on the rim of Bryce Canyon, Ruby knew they would be successful building a new inn at the entrance to the new national monument. He was sure that he was located on the best route to Bryce Canyon and donated 15 acres of his land to build the new road. His neighbors thought this was not wise, as he divided his property in half, but he knew this would insure the future success of his inn.

The sign at Ruby's Inn reads, "Everybody welcome." Ruby Syrett is shown (right) with Dr. W. H. Hopkins, a dentist from Salt Lake City. Dr. Hopkins became a great promoter of Bryce Canyon and Ruby's Inn. He was an avid photographer and submitted many of his images to the newspapers in the West, as well as wrote detailed articles explaining how one could visit the area.

The inn continued to expand. Local timber was used to build the log structure that was attached to the original plank building. Ponderosa pine was abundant, and sawmills were close, allowing for a constant supply of building materials.

Visitors continued to arrive seeking lodging and meals. This group of visitors from around 1928 paused to have a picture taken with Ruby (left).

As automobile travel became more popular, the need to provide fuel became necessary. In the beginning, Ruby had to drive about 80 miles to Marysvale to fill 55-gallon drums with gasoline and return to the inn. Eventually, they could also provide oil and tires to the traveler. Note the hand pump in front of the inn.

In the beginning, guest accommodations were sparse. Small tent cabins were constructed with wooden floors, half walls, and a canvas tent cover. This type of lodging was very popular with the stream of "tin can tourists" taking to the newly constructed roadways being developed to connect Utah's new national parks.

As demand increased, so did the quality of the cabins. Shown here are wooden cabins that provided additional comfort to the traveler. Early advertisements offered a cabin with springs from $1 to $2.50 per day. Camping privileges were available at 50¢ per car for the first day and 25¢ each additional day, with wood and water included.

Camping was very popular, and many travelers were equipped with all the necessities, which were usually tied to the car and easily accessible for setting up camp or stopping for the noon meal, often prepared over a fire on the side of the road.

Carl Syrett (left) is pictured here with his father Ruby in front of the inn. As Carl worked with his father, he began to take on more responsibilities. He took care of the outside, including the farming and livestock, and Ruby greeted the guests and was in charge of the inside portion of the business.

Fire was always a threat at the inn. This c. 1935 photograph shows the cleanup of a fire that destroyed the light plant behind the inn. It was attributed to a spark from the light switch that ignited gasoline being stored in the same building. In the winter of 1923, a storage building containing all of the supplies for the new inn burned to the ground. Another fire destroyed the sawmill with all of its equipment, including the planer, a shingle mill, and all of the lumber. A separate fire destroyed about 60 tons of hay, the critical feed for wintering the livestock.

This image shows Theron Griffin as a young man in front of the inn. From the beginning, Ruby's Inn was noted for the Western experience. Theron entertained guests at the inn.

RUBY'S INN — NEAR ENTRANCE TO BRYCE CANYON NATIONAL PARK, UTAH

This 1930s vintage postcard shows the continued expansion of services at the inn, as well as the changes in automobiles of the time.

In this photograph, Ruby's Inn sports a new balcony addition. Note that the designs of the cars continued to change, and some of the gas pumps are now automatic. A customer could now pump gas without actually having to "pump" the gas.

Does this look natural to you

This late-1940s photograph shows the continued improvements, including air-conditioning. Note the screen doors on each room. Ruby's Inn had always provided meals for its customers, but now it had a full-service café. Ruby also became the postmaster, and a post office was available, which continues to operate today.

WHILE VISITING BRYCE CANYON NAT'L PARK STOP AT RUBY'S INN. UTAH. OPEN ALL YEAR. ROOMS. MODERN. HEATED.

RUBY'S INN NEAR BRYCE CANYON NAT'L PARK ON HIGHWAY NO. 12 OFF HIGHWAY NO. 89. ROOM WITH BATH $3.00   G-567

This postcard captures Ruby and Minnie doing what they did best: welcoming visitors to Ruby's Inn and beautiful Bryce Canyon. Note that, by now, they were able to offer rooms with a bath for $3 a night.

The inn continues to look much the same, but the styles of the cars keep changing. The roads continued to improve, and the time to reach a destination became shorter. This allowed the visitation to continue to increase from a few hundred visitors in the beginning to thousands by the early 1950s.

This business-advertising card shows how things have changed. Note the "Meat Sandwich" is 15¢, or 25¢ if served on a plate at a table. Ruby used to say that a meat sandwich should always have more meat than bread. It also shows a "Shower Bath" being sold separately.

RUBY'S INN
OPEN ALL YEAR

Three and a half miles this side of
Beautiful Bryce Canyon
Beauty Salon and Barber Service

Regular Meals, Lunches, Beds, Campers' Supplies, Fresh Milk, Butter, Eggs, and Bread.
PRICES RIGHT

Garage Service   Cars Stored 50c
GAS - OILS - ACCESSORIES - ETC.

Saddle Horses, Guides, for Side Trips AND PLENTY OF PLACES TO GO!

For Reservation: Address
R. C. SYRETT, P. O. Ruby's Inn, Utah

AAA

RATES AT RUBY'S INN
FAIR PRICES TO ALL

Meat Sandwich	15c
Served on plate at table	25c
No table service less than	25c
Waffles and Coffee	30c
Second Order	20c
Bed for one person	$1.25
Bed, 2 in same bed	$2.00
Breakfast	25c to 75c
Lunch	35c to 75c
Dinner	75c to $1.00
One-fourth Pie	10c
Whole Pie	40c
Milk, quart	15c
Eggs	Market price
Shower Bath	25c
Saddle Horses, per day	$2.50
Cabin with Springs, $1 to 2.50 per day	

EXCELLENT CAMP GROUNDS
Camping privileges 50c per car 1st day 25c each additional day, wood and water included

A place away up in the Pines that calls to memory that Beautiful song:
HOME SWEET HOME

OPEN ALL YEAR

By the late 1950s, the inn was becoming known all over the world. Services continued to be updated with conveniences for the traveler. The inn added an electric sign and a modern phone for anyone who wanted to make a call.

Children learned to work at an early age at the inn. Armeda Syrett (left) is pictured helping her mother, Minnie. The family worked hard in all aspects of the business, with Minnie supervising the housekeeping, front desk, and café. From the time Carl and Armeda were old enough to stir the pan, they helped with the laundry, which was washed in a large open vat with a fire underneath for heat. They made their own lye soap to do the wash. As the tourists continued to increase, many local young people came to work for the summer. Minnie trained and supervised them. She sometimes referred to the young girls in her charge as "her little dam its," as they were always full of surprises. One story tells of a young girl who was asked to clean the silver and instructed to use plenty of elbow grease. When Minnie returned to check on her progress, nothing was done. When asked why, the girl explained that she could not find the elbow grease.

The café was a favorite with the guests. There was always plenty to eat and a wide selection on the menu. Minnie was very fussy about her dining room and insisted that fresh tablecloths and napkins were always in place. She also liked to provide fresh flowers when they were available and added touches such as Western art and natural arrangements in baskets. Ice cream and root beer were also very popular with the guests.

When Ruby cut the cedar posts for the construction of the inn, he left the branches sticking out, and they were used to hang a coat or hat. In spite of the chilly climate on the plateau, large wood stoves kept the dining room warm and inviting.

The spacious lobby at Ruby's Inn was designed to allow guests to relax and enjoy one another's company after spending the day at Bryce Canyon. It featured large windows, allowing the natural light to brighten the room during the day, and electric lights for the night. Originally, the inn was lit with kerosene lamps. Later, the Syretts used carbide lamps before building their own electric plant to generate the electricity for the inn.

The rustic flavor of the lobby was enhanced by the hickory-and-wicker furniture arranged throughout. Guests spent the evenings in conversation, playing cards, and sharing their impressions of Bryce Canyon. Occasionally, dances were held to celebrate a holiday or other special occasion and an orchestra would be recruited.

The most prominent feature in the lobby was a huge stone fireplace. It was constructed of local materials that were gathered and placed into the rockwork. Ruby and Carl brought back specimens of petrified wood, dinosaur bone, and fossils that were also imbedded in the mortar. Utilizing these unusual specimens, they fashioned a message to their guests, spelling out the invitation to "Tell Your Friends About Me." Another continuing theme of welcoming their guests is spelled out using manzanita branches, which grew nearby. The large collections of Navajo rugs were acquired from Navajo men who came each fall to trade their blankets for horses or money.

This picture shows the recently completed fireplace. Restrooms were eventually built on either side, and the windows were no longer visible. Note the construction of the roof in the rear of the fireplace. No insulation was used, and daylight was seen between the walls and the roof boards. Also shown above the fireplace is another example of how Minnie used local materials to decorate the inn and invite the guests to feel "Welcome."

Ruby insisted on always having a fire burning in the fireplace. If the fire got to low, he would say, "Put another log on the fire, we have plenty of wood." Over the years, many stories were shared around this wonderful fireplace, and visitors from around the world told their friends back home about it.

Snow comes early to the high plateaus. At an elevation of 7,600 feet, the growing season is short, and the winters can be long. Snow would blanket the inn and cover the roads, sometimes isolating the inn for days at a time. Note the second-story windows that are nearly covered with snow and the high drifts in the front. A group of girls stands on the roof, enjoying the crisp winter day.

When the roads were closed, mail and supplies were moved with a team and sleigh. Ruby is seen loading the sleigh and preparing to rendezvous with the mail truck. In harsh weather, deliveries were made to a box located at the junction on the main highway. Ruby and the postal driver each had a key.

Deep snow made car travel unsafe, if not impossible. With few tourists on the road, the inn slowed down, and the family settled in for a rest. As seen here, practical use of covered spaces were utilized to store supplies and even the car for the winter. It was many years before plows were available to keep the roads cleared of the deep, drifting snow.

When the snow got too deep, it required getting on the roof and shoveling. This hard work was necessary to prevent damage to the structure. The family recalls the story of Ruby having a dream that the roof was going to fall in. He got up immediately, inspected the structure, and found a crack in a main beam. He was able to add support and avoid a dangerous collapse.

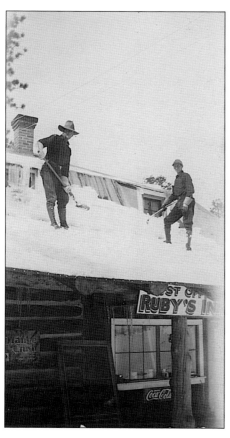

Ruby (left) and Carl are shown shoveling the roof of the inn.

Ruby and Minnie show the depth of the snow on the sides of the road. In those days, winter travel was slow at best and sometimes life-threatening. Many stories are told of mountain rescues of travelers who were caught in the sudden winter storms.

Pictured here are, from left to right, Carl Syrett, his wife, Thelma, and their daughter Mary, and Minnie and Ruby on a bright winter day.

The warm days of winter allow the snow to melt and water to move through the formations. The extreme cold of the winter nights causes the water to freeze, continuing the sculpting of nature on the limestone formations of Bryce Canyon.

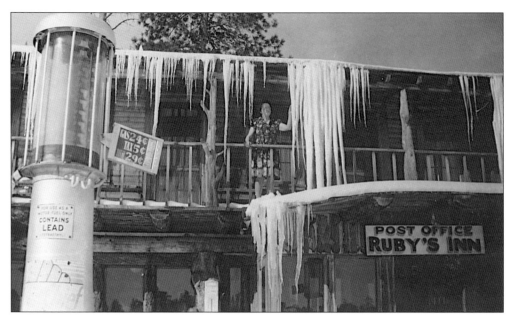

The same freezing and thawing can be seen in the icicles dwarfing Minnie on the balcony of the inn.

Minnie is shown in waist-high snow as she walks to the line where she hangs the laundry in the warmer months of the year.

Long winter shadows appear as Ruby, his granddaughter Mary, and Thelma return to the inn.

An image of a winter outing shows friends exploring Mossy Cave. Water seeps in this natural grotto and provides a cool retreat for visitors in the summer. In winter, it is transformed to a mass of giant icicles attached to the roof of the shallow cave.

In this c. 1942 image, Ruby Syrett is seen on the rim of Bryce Canyon. One may wonder if he is reflecting on his life and unique connection to this beautiful part of the natural world. It has been 30-plus years since Ruby, his wife, Minnie, and their small family had first witnessed the indescribable beauty of Bryce Canyon. Providing friendship and warm hospitality to the increasing number of visitors had become his life's work.

Ruby and Minnie were truly partners, not only in marriage, but in all that they did. They worked together to build a lasting legacy, not just the inn that bore his name, but the family that continued to believe in the same notions of hard work along with sincere western hospitality.

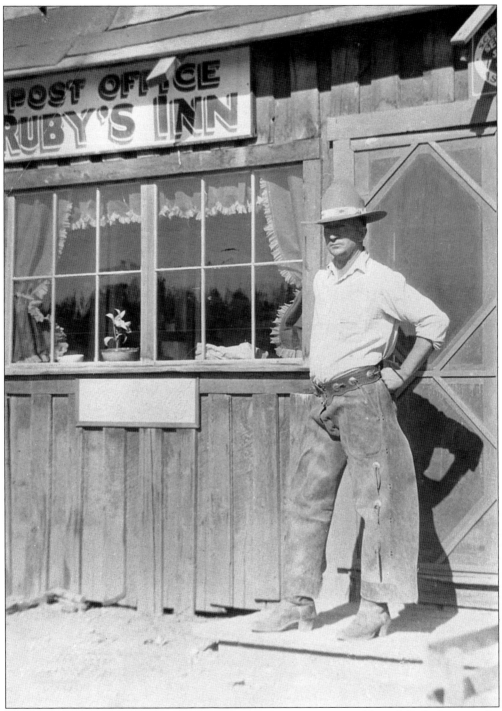

By the late 1920s, Ruby's Inn was providing everything a visitor could need. Ruby became the postmaster of Ruby's Inn and provided mail service to his guests as well as neighbors in the surrounding area. This also allowed Ruby's Inn to be included on maps of the time. Ruby's Inn was becoming more than just a tourist lodging—it was becoming a destination.

By the early 1930s, visitors to Bryce Canyon were not only seeking the wonders of Mother Nature, they wanted to experience a bit of the West. Ruby is shown in front of the inn preparing to guide his guests by horseback, leaving the tourist roads, and for a short time, letting them spend time with a real cowboy.

Armeda Syrett came to Bryce Canyon when she was just six weeks old. She grew up experiencing the pioneering efforts of her parents in the company of her elder brother Carl. From their youth, they helped with the work and welcomed visitors to Ruby's Inn. Armeda married LeGrande Farnsworth, and they spent their first years together working at the inn. They later moved away and reared a family of five children.

This group of men includes J.W. Humphrey (left), Wallace N. Roundy (center, holding a coat), and Ruby Syrett (second from right). The rest are unidentified. They are clearly in a formal pose and may be concluding a meeting of one of the many civic groups or boards that Ruby served on. By the late 1930s, providing good roads and electricity had become the focus of many of the leaders in this remote part of Southern Utah.

Ruby and Minnie Syrett (center) take a moment to have a picture taken with unidentified friends or guests in about 1940. The Syretts often received letters and photographs from folks who had been their guests at the inn. In those early days, reservations were requested by letter, and often, correspondence continued as friends, inquiring about family as well as availability of rooms for a future stay.

John Thompson, a handyman, worked for years at the inn. He came to the area with the Civilian Conservation Corps workers, married a local girl, and raised his family in Panguitch. They spent their summers living at the inn and, like many others, moved back to town in the fall so their children could attend school.

This early-1950s image shows Hart Johnson (left) and a friend enjoying the warmth of the famous fireplace in the lobby of the inn. Johnson was a jovial fellow, and the Syrett family has fond memories of his joking antics. Johnson worked doing odd jobs and helped with the livestock and the farm. He resided in Cannonville, Utah. He and two friends were in an accident in the desert west of town, where their vehicle rolled over the edge of Bull Valley Gorge, a 200-foot-deep slot canyon; none of them survived.

Early in the 1930s, Ruby built a studio for Hal Rumel, an artist and photographer from Salt Lake City. This was a time when commercial photography utilizing color was in its infancy. Rumel spent his days capturing the images of Bryce Canyon, processing the prints, and selling them to the tourists at the inn. He went on to become a well-known and respected commercial photographer residing in Salt Lake City.

This is another view of the Bryce Studio. This structure was located just south of the inn. Guests could walk over and view the new color photographs as well as a selection of traditional black-and-white images.

This late-1930s photograph shows Rumel (right) with his wife Lenessa and their family. The Rumels spent the summers of their early married life living at Bryce Canyon. They shared in the labors and would be seen washing their photographic plates in the nearby stream. Many of the early postcards of the Bryce Canyon area bear his name.

Jack Rheinhart, a dance instructor from California, brought students to perform and provide entertainment for the many visitors to the area in the summer. He also included local young people who wanted to learn and join the group. Note the changes to the inn, including the addition of a walkway to access the rooms on the second level. This photograph was taken prior to the installation of the railings.

This c. 1930s photograph shows Jack Rheinhart's students posing on one of the trails below the rim of Bryce Canyon. Rheinhart is front right, and Armeda Syrett is second on the left. Rheinhart taught a variety of dance and was well known for his Spanish dancing.

During the summer, entertainment was provided for the guests at the inn. It included slide shows, dances with big bands, and, of course, singing cowboys like Theron Griffin (left), Herman Pollock

(center), and Karl Webb.

Tourists, like this unidentified girl, loved the cowboys. They enjoyed the music, and they all wanted to have a picture taken with them. Herm Pollock commented about this photograph, "Why, that girl came all the way from Paris, France." That trend has continued, and tourists still want pictures taken with the cowboys as they continue to come from all over the world. Identified, from left to right, are Theron Griffin, Karl Webb, and Herman Pollock.

Four

RUBY'S INN

By 1930, many important events had taken place that forever changed the future of Bryce Canyon. The roads were improved from the Grand Canyon Highway (US Highway 89), and the tunnels were completed in Red Canyon on June 1, 1925. Bryce Canyon was proclaimed a national park on September 15, 1928. The year 1930 also saw the completion of the tunnels through Zion, allowing a connection with Mount Carmel, Utah. These improvements assured that visitors could travel between Bryce, Zion, and the North Rim of the Grand Canyon.

Ruby and Minnie Syretts' business continued to grow to meet the increasing need. They added rooms with heat and a bath. Electric lights replaced kerosene and carbide, and gas and oil were available for the travelers. The café was expanded, and Western entertainment provided. Horse trips to new regions proved popular, and the inn stayed open all year.

This serene c. 1924 image was made at the home of Dr. W.H. Hopkins in Salt Lake City during the Christmas holiday. It shows, from left to right, Dr. Hopkins's sister, Minnie, Ruby Syrett, Anna Hopkins, Armeda, and Carl Syrett. The Syretts and Dr. Hopkins had an enduring friendship from the early days of Tourists Rest to the untimely death of Ruby on May 8, 1945.

A young Armeda Syrett enjoys a warm spring day at her family's home around 1920. Note that the family car is still covered to provide protection from the late snowstorms that frequent the high plateau region. Armeda and her brother Carl grew up without close neighbors and relied on each other for friendship. Armeda had many fond memories of those times growing up at Ruby's Inn.

Armeda Syrett and her niece Mary are seen in front of one of the guest cabins at Ruby's Inn. The garden is protected by chicken wire, though it was not necessary to keep the chickens out; rather, it provided a defense against the herds of deer.

Pictured here in about 1930, young Mary, daughter of Carl and Thelma Syrett, was Ruby and Minnie's first grandchild. Carl and Thelma Alvey were married June 20, 1928. Thelma had grown up in Escalante, Utah, situated 50 miles to the east of Ruby's Inn. Note the rustic cabins that were built to accommodate the ever-growing demand for lodging at Bryce Canyon.

Mary is seen sitting on a road grader that was pulled by a team of horses. Ruby used this equipment to level the ground, build roads, and construct the runway at the Bryce Canyon Airport. This old grader still sits in a place of honor outside the post office and general store at Ruby's Inn.

Mary often tested her sliding skills in front of the inn. The inn stayed open year-round to take care of the few visitors braving the winter conditions and visiting Bryce. This also provided a welcome opportunity to share stories and news while enjoying a hot meal and the warmth of a roaring fire.

Ruby's grandsons Phil (left) and Carl Farnsworth practice their cowboy skills. Riding, roping, and catching the bad guys was what all young cowboys wanted to do. There was ample opportunity for young minds to imagine the cowboy ways and spend time with their grandfather, who had really lived that life.

This early-1930s photograph was probably taken during a traditional late-spring birthday celebration for Armeda. She once explained that they would always go into the woods surrounding the inn and prepare a Dutch-oven dinner. Pictured, from left to right, are Thelma Syrett, Minnie, Carl, Mary, and Armeda.

This photograph shows Jean Bybee Syrett (left) and Mary. Jean became Carl's second wife after the sudden passing of Thelma on August 5, 1939. Jean had worked at the inn and helped take care of Carl and Thelma's children.

Seen here, the Syrett and Farnsworth cousins try to pose for a portrait. From left to right are Carl Farnsworth, Phil Farnsworth, Arthur Syrett, Mary, Doug Syrett, and Dawnetta Syrett.

This picture was taken shortly after the death of Carl's wife, Thelma, in August 1939. From left to right are Carl, Doug, Mary, Dawnetta, Minnie, Arthur, Ruby, Phil, and Armeda Syrett. This was a time of great sadness for the young father, who lost his wife, and his children, who lost their mother. (Courtesy of Hal Rumel.)

Carl Syrett and Jean (Bybee) Syrett were married on November 19, 1940. Carl had four children, and together, he and Jean had six more, making a family of 10 children to raise and care for. From the very beginning, Jean loved and nurtured Carl's children as her own and worked all of her life to provide a sense of security to all of their children.

This early-1930s image shows the family and extended family on a rare warm-weather trip. Because the summer was when they needed to be at the inn and take care of business, pictures showing relaxation often also showed snow. Restaurants were scarce along the way, so meals were often served picnic-style.

Ruby and Minnie overlook the canyon that was spanned by the new Grand Canyon Bridge. The bridge was completed in January 1929 and connected the states of Utah and Arizona. This connection replaced Lees Ferry, built in 1873, which provided the only crossing of the river. It would have taken over 600 miles to go around that crossing.

With the completion of the bridge and the Grand Canyon Highway from Panguitch to Kanab, travelers were able to venture forth and discover the wonders of the North Rim of the Grand Canyon. This 1920 photograph shows a well-equipped traveler parked in front of the ranger station at Jacobs Lake.

The license plate on the car dates this photograph from 1923. The image seems to be in front of one of the tourist facilities on the Arizona section of the Kaibab Plateau. The facility must be fairly new, as there are plentiful wood chips in the foreground. Hardy folks of all ages enjoyed the spirit of adventure afforded by these early road trips.

By the early 1920s, roads connecting the now famous destinations were not always easy to travel. One needed to be prepared, as there were often no other travelers to stop and offer assistance.

Many motorists found the deep sands of Monument Valley to be more of an obstacle than men with shovels could overcome. More horsepower was what was needed, as demonstrated in this c. 1918 photograph.

Pictured is an early automobile on the road through Marysvale Canyon. Note the railroad tracks along the hill in the background. Marysvale was as far south as the railroad extended along the Sevier River Valley of Central Utah. This road eventually became US Highway 89, allowing north-to-south, border-to-border travel through the state.

Sometimes one had to use his imagination to see the road through Utah's slick rock country. These daring travelers must have felt a great spirit of adventure, as well as accomplishment, when they arrived at their destination in about 1918.

From 1873 until June 1927, the only means of traversing the Colorado River was an automobile crossing at Lee's Ferry, seen in this c. 1918 image. When the ferry sank in an accident and three men were killed, it was never replaced since the New Grand Canyon Bridge was nearing completion.

Crossing the rugged Utah canyons seemed to continually challenge the road builders. The recently completed Hell's Backbone Bridge, built by the Civilian Conservation Corps in the 1930s, connected the towns of Escalante and Boulder in Utah. It crosses a chasm that drops 1,500 feet to the canyon floor.

Pictured here is a bridge crossing the wash at Water Canyon. This is the so-called Dump Road (Utah Highway 12), named for the irrigation water that dumps off the rim of Bryce Canyon and provides water to the farms of Bryce Valley below. The road climbs about 1,000 feet and connects the valley with the plateau on top. The road is so steep, many of the early automobiles had to go up backwards, as they did not have fuel pumps and depended entirely on gravity.

All of the roads in Southern Utah were not located in the desert; some made their way through the alpine forests of the higher country. This photograph of a 1920s road trip shows just how dedicated some of these early explorers needed to be. Some left their marks by carving their initials in the quaking aspens seen to the right.

When it came time to eat, it came time to stop. Meals were cooked on the fire, and stories of the day were shared as travelers took time to rest. Dr. W.H. Hopkins (right), his wife Anna (seated, center), and unidentified friends take time to share the shade of a giant ponderosa pine.

This 1920 scene seems to be along the Sevier River on the way to or from Bryce Canyon. Dr. Hopkins is in the background and is bringing the water from the river, and his unidentified friend is cooking their meal.

Dr. Hopkins (left), a dentist from Salt Lake City, sits with his close friend L.D. Phouts, a dentist from Payson, Utah. The license plate on the motorcycle bears a 1918 date. This was an exciting way to travel as a passenger had to ride in the sidecar.

Roads continued to improve, making travel much easier, as well as faster, for the Bryce Canyon visitor. This car travels along the newly graded road in Red Canyon.

On June 1, 1925, Utah governor George Dern led a caravan of 315 cars to celebrate the opening of the Utah National Park, later named Bryce Canyon. He was met with a closed gate at the tunnels in Red Canyon and greeted by many of the children of Panguitch, dressed as brownies and fairies. They proceeded to tie ribbons to the bumper of his car, and when he proclaimed that he did indeed believe in fairies, the gates were opened and they were invited to proceed to Utah's Fairyland.

This 1918 photograph shows the Eureka, Utah, Boy Scout Troop 1 lining up in front of the Red Canyon Tunnel. The Scouts are on their way to set up camp at what would become Bryce Canyon National Park.

This enthusiastic group has traveled to Bryce Canyon from Salt Lake City. The photograph was taken in 1923, the last season of operation for the Syretts' lodge on the canyon rim.

Automobiles were not the only means of exploring the canyons. Ruby kept a number of saddle horses for tourists looking for adventure away from crowds. Claude Sudweeks of Tropic, a cousin of Ruby, was the one who invited Ruby and Minnie to see the big "hole in the ground." Sudweeks helped Ruby guide many of those horse trips.

Ruby waters horses at the White Man Springs. Note the hewn logs that have been fashioned to hold the water. This spring is used today by wildlife and livestock. Remnants of the troughs can still be seen.

In the winter months, Ruby needed to travel to the lower desert country to check on his livestock. This area was in the lower Paria River drainage and much lower in elevation than the plateau. Often, Ruby took customers on these pack trips and let them experience the unique landscape on horseback. This photograph was taken at a cowboy shelter called the "Monkey House." It was situated between large boulders and enclosed by rocks on the sides.

In this 1920 image, Dr. Hopkins sits horseback on a formation that he named the "Pyramid." He wrote an article that appears in the *Salt Lake Tribune* Sunday magazine dated May 8, 1921. It is entitled "No Man's Land: a Journey by Pack Train into the Land of Mystery." This same area that captured his imagination has become the Grand Staircase-Escalante National Monument.

Dr. Hopkins (left) and Ruby are seen in front of what the ranchers called the "post office." Located on the lower Paria River, it features unusual erosion in the sandstone walls. The name came from the tradition of cattlemen leaving supplies and messages for fellow ranchers as they returned from trips to town. Men would be away from home for a month or six weeks at a time while they took care of their livestock during the winter months.

In about 1920, Dr. Hopkins (right) and Carl Syrett explore ancient structures left by the early inhabitants of the area.

Lone Rock, situated on the lower Paria River, was a landmark used by travelers and cattlemen as a point of reference, as well as a meeting place. From early pioneer days, the only road connecting Cannonville and the town of Paria went through this riverbed. Winter was the best season to be in this lower country, avoiding the heat and flash floods of summer.

The pack train has stopped for the explorers to view the desert expanses as it breaks away from the slick rock ledges of this rugged country. Those few who had the chance to join these unique trips were able to experience a vanishing way of life. In return for the effort required by a city dweller to endure this harsh country were memories that would last a lifetime.

Ruby leads the train out of the canyon, ending another adventure into this remote yet spectacular region of Utah's Canyon Country.

Five

THE THIRD GENERATION

Change had always been part of the Ruby's Inn story, and the 1970s began an era of continued building and expansion that continues today. Carl and Jean Syrett had retired. Many of the Syrett children, who had grown up working and learning the business, wanted to stay and contribute to the future of the inn. They soon realized that they would need to expand their business in order to provide for their growing families. That realization began a journey for Ruby and Minnie's grandchildren that would span over 40 years. Working together as a family, they expanded the business, raised their own families, experienced hardship and joy, and are able to look back knowing they gave their all to continue Ruby's dream. The Syrett family is now seeing members of the fourth and fifth generations working and learning the business in preparation for carrying on the legacy of Ruby's Inn. Ruby and Minnie would be very proud.

This 1980s photograph shows the progressive changes that had taken place at the inn. New buildings were added, providing additional guest rooms. In 1976, the inn became part of the Best Western hotel chain.

Carl and Jean Syrett retired in 1979. They looked forward to spending time traveling and catching up on fishing. Jean claimed she did not really enjoy fishing but was grateful for the time she was able to spend with Carl.

Carl, his sons, and son-in-law are pictured in this August 6, 1967, photograph taken the day after Rod and Kathren Syrett's wedding. Shown, from left to right, are Fred, Rod, Bob, Mondell, Arthur, and Doug Syrett, Craig Rutledge, and Carl Syrett.

Jean (Bybee) Syrett is pictured on August 6, 1967, with her daughters and daughters-in-law. Shown, from left to right, are Jean Syrett, Dawnetta Rutledge, Marianne, Florence, Kathern, Shauna, and Karleen Syrett.

On the night of May 31, 1984, a fire destroyed the original old lodge, 19 guest rooms, and the new restaurant. Firemen responded from Tropic, Bryce Canyon, Panguitch, and other surrounding areas to help fight the blaze. The glow of the fire could be seen for miles around, and many reported the profound sadness they felt when they learned it was Ruby's Inn.

When daylight allowed an inspection of the building, the Syrett family realized it was a total, catastrophic loss. The monetary loss was over $4 million, and the emotional loss was overwhelming. Countless items collected by Ruby and Minnie that meant so much to the family, including the original lobby and fireplace, were completely destroyed. This was the beginning of the tourist season. Employees needed to work, and guests needed to be taken care of, so there was no time to waste. With the same pioneer fortitude that guided Ruby and Minnie, the family and their employees and friends went to work to rebuild the inn. Within three weeks, a temporary restaurant had been built, and guests continued to come.

Working through the summer crowds and winter snow, Ruby's Inn reopened on June 1, 1985, one year after the fire. The new inn incorporated many of the things that Ruby had built into his original inn. Log posts and rough-hewn trusses were designed into the lobby. Logs were used throughout. Log siding and stone were used on the exterior, and many of the historical photographs and antiques were again used to tell the Bryce Canyon story. The general store was expanded, and a large meeting room was also included.

Water was always needed at the inn. During the 1980s, a new well was drilled, and storage tanks were installed to provide a dependable supply of culinary water. A sewer system was also constructed. The third generation of the family was willing to commit to whatever was required to improve and continue building for the future.

Seen here is Best Western Plus Ruby's Inn today. The main lodge is the hub of all of the activity at Ruby's Inn. Included in the lodge are a spacious lobby and hotel registration, the Cowboy's Buffet & Steak Room, Ruby's Inn General Store, Old West Photos, Minnie's Beauty Salon, large

conference rooms, enclosed indoor access to guest rooms, and a large indoor pool. All of the latest amenities are available, including cable television and Wi-Fi.

The Ruby's Inn lobby is spacious and includes a large fireplace. Incorporated into the stonework is the message that Ruby and Minnie had offered from the very beginning: "Welcome." Times have changed, but the idea of providing travelers with comfortable accommodations, hot meals, and friendly service continues to be the goal of the family.

The dining room replicates the comfortable feeling of the old lodge. Horseshoe hangers take the place of the tree limbs, but guests can still feel free to hang their coats or hats. The restaurant offers a buffet or full menu and can accommodate both small and large groups.

The Canyon Diner provides the traveler with a fine selection of great Western fast food.

The Bryce Canyon Car Care Center is a full-service fuel station, automotive, and RV repair and car, truck, and bus wash, as well as a provider of propane and RV dump facilities.

The new Best Western Bryce Canyon Grand Hotel is located across the street from Ruby's Inn. It was built in 2008 to provide guests with the very best in upscale hotel amenities. It includes an indoor courtyard with pool and spa, fitness center, business center, guest laundry, meeting rooms, and a full hot-breakfast buffet. The 161 guest rooms are deluxe and tastefully designed for convenience and comfort.

Bryce View Lodge, also located across the street from Ruby's Inn, provides 160 moderately priced guest rooms. All of the facilities of the inn are available to the Bryce View Lodge guests.

Ebenezer's Barn and Grill opened in 2008. The name is a tribute to Ebenezer Bryce, for whom the canyon was named.

The Bar G Wranglers perform nightly, seven nights a week, from the first of May to mid-October. The cowboy entertainment is reminiscent of the cowboys who provided the Western experience for those early visitors to Bryce Canyon.

The Old Bryce Town Shops were constructed in the late 1980s to provide the visitor with another type of Western experience. Designed to have the look and feel of a Western town, it offers gift shops, hand-dipped ice cream, a rock shop, a faux jail, and an old mill.

The Ruby's Inn Express runs during the summer season and provides connections to the lodging, restaurants, shopping, rodeo, Ebenezer's Barn and Grill, and the campground.

Horseback rides continue the tradition started by Ruby of providing tours to the rim of Bryce Canyon, as well as one-half- and all-day rides in Red Canyon. Nightly rodeos are also enjoyed from May through August, Wednesday through Saturday nights.

Guided ATV tours are available during the summer months, providing visitors the opportunity to view the rim of Bryce Canyon and follow trails through the Dixie National Forest. Rides are one hour, half day, and all day.

Camping has forever been popular with visitors to Bryce Canyon. Ruby always had a place for travelers to set up their tents and enjoy camping under the pines. In 1988, a new campground was developed, including over 200 sites for recreational vehicle and tent campers. Small cabins and tipis were also available for reservation. The new campground provided a swimming pool and spa, as well as showers and guest laundry, to round out the camping experience.

Ruby's Inn remains open through the winter months, providing services to those hardy folks who want to miss the crowds and experience Bryce Canyon in its beautiful snow-covered splendor. Winter activities include cross-country skiing, ice-skating, and horse-drawn sleigh rides. Ski and skate rentals are also available.

In the early days, deep snow on the high plateaus sometimes closed roads, and considerable effort was needed to remove it. Today, heavy equipment has made this season much easier to enjoy, and travel is much safer. The roads inside Bryce are kept open throughout the winter, allowing visitors to experience this beautiful season of the year.

The Bryce Canyon Shuttle operates throughout the summer to provide a convenient alternative to driving into the park. The service is included in the cost of the park pass and allows visitors to leave their vehicles parked at the shuttle staging area outside the park. Convenient shuttle stops are also available for the hotel and campground guests.

Ruby's dream of providing the best in facilities and services to Bryce Canyon visitors was realized when the area around Ruby's Inn was incorporated in August 2007, becoming Bryce Canyon City. In a few short years, roads have been improved, a staging area for the shuttle was constructed, and a main street improvement project is being planned for the spring of 2013. With these changes, a stoplight will be installed, the first one in Garfield County.

This 2012 photograph shows the newly completed regional public safety facility built in Bryce Canyon City. This project houses fire, emergency response, ambulance, and search-and-rescue equipment for the town and Garfield County. With this facility, a new volunteer fire department was organized to help provide the necessary fire protection for all of the structures on the plateau.

Ruby and Minnie Syrett began their story in 1916 when they moved their family to Bryce Canyon. They worked together to raise their family, build their business and welcome visitors to their inn. Their children Carl and Armeda would continue the journey as they grew up at the inn. Armeda and her husband, LeGrande, would spend their early married years working together with Carl, Jean, Ruby and Minnie. Eventually Armeda's family would move to begin a new life away from the inn, and Carl and Jean would continue working at the inn. Carl would take over the position of postmaster that Ruby had begun so many years before. They raised their family at the inn in the summers, returning to Panguitch in the autumns for school.

Pictured, from left to right, are LeGrande and Armeda Farnsworth, and Jean and Carl Syrett.

W.H. Hopkins was a dentist from Salt Lake City, self-proclaimed world traveler, and unwavering supporter of Bryce Canyon National Park. He took the time to make many of these photographs and through a series of small, miraculous events, they continue to exist today. He shared with Ruby and Minnie their vision for hosting visitors to the canyons. He remained a lifelong friend.

DISCOVER THOUSANDS OF LOCAL HISTORY BOOKS FEATURING MILLIONS OF VINTAGE IMAGES

Arcadia Publishing, the leading local history publisher in the United States, is committed to making history accessible and meaningful through publishing books that celebrate and preserve the heritage of America's people and places.

Find more books like this at
www.arcadiapublishing.com

Search for your hometown history, your old stomping grounds, and even your favorite sports team.

Consistent with our mission to preserve history on a local level, this book was printed in South Carolina on American-made paper and manufactured entirely in the United States. Products carrying the accredited Forest Stewardship Council (FSC) label are printed on 100 percent FSC-certified paper.

MADE IN THE